Dr. JAC's ™

Writing
Workshop
Primer
Reading

Dr. JAC's

Reading
Writing
Workshop
Primer

Joyce Armstrong Carroll
Ed.D., H.L.D

Absey & Co.
Spring, Texas

Permissions
Absey & Co. Inc.
23011 Northcrest
Spring, TX 77389
888-412-2739

ISBN 1-888842-44-X

Designed by Edward E. Wilson

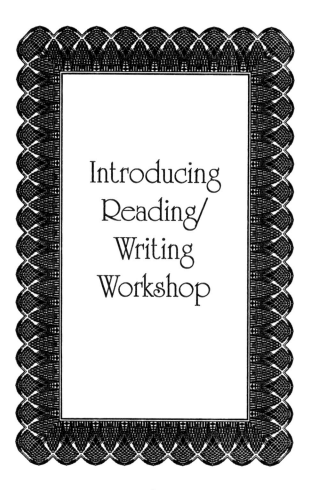

Introducing
Reading/
Writing
Workshop

In order to truly teach reading and writing effectively, to enable choice, and to foster independence, training in and support for the reading/ writing workshop (hereafter called workshop) is a logical step, a step usually taken after teachers have been trained in the teaching of reading and writing as processes. The purpose of workshop is to integrate reading with all its attendant skills with writing and its attendant skills into a meaningful context. This integration energizes generative time on task for students and individualized instructional time for teachers. If well planned and consistently executed, it best fits the needs of learners and frees teachers to facilitate, monitor, and teach most productively.

Workshop helps teachers move away from every day, all day whole class instruction. In the whole class instructional environment, all too often:

• the students in one sub group, generally the average group, have their needs met;

• the students in another sub group, those who have already learned the material, are left to look for ways to occupy their time;

• students in a third sub group, finding themselves utterly lost, become bored or mischievous, learning little or nothing.

Further, workshop moves students away from dependence upon the teacher for every move made in the classroom. It weans young students away from the "Miss, is this right?" "Miss, I'm finished. What do I do now?" syndrome to more independence. It provides a structure for older students within which to make decisions without overwhelming them with all the possibilities. Proper teacher guidance enables student to experience freedom with direction without having to do everything.

As Wiggins and McTighe state in *Understanding by Design*, "We believe schoolwork itself can be designed to be far more interesting without sacrificing rigor. Schoolwork is often needlessly boring, especially when composed of mind-numbing skill worksheets or excessive passive listening—all of it divorced from interesting problems and realistic performance challenges" (119).

Workshop presents an intelligent alternative to this problem by eliminating mindlessness and passivity while offering genuine challenges.

A caveat:

Workshop is not the only way to teach reading and writing, but it is a powerful and effective way.

Defining
Reading/
Writing
Workshop

Like so many terms in education, the term *workshop* often connotes different meanings, idiosyncratic nuances, misinterpretations, and loose applications. Therefore, *workshop* begs for definition.

Quite simply, workshop is a daily time frame in which students and teachers make decisions about learning and teaching. Students' needs and the teachers' determinations shape the learning time in compatible and important ways. Choice plays an important role in workshop as do clear objectives. Only when both students and teachers together undertake the responsibility for learning does true ownership for both take place.

Workshop consists of
* **Minilessons**—short lessons that set forth the concept, clarify the concept, reteach the concept, or serve some purpose set by the teacher when assessing the needs of the students.

* **Microminilessons**—shorter lessons of the above.

* **Status-of-the-class**—a term originated by Nanci Atwell that describes the poll the teacher takes of each student regarding his or her goal for workshop that day.

* **One-on-one reading**—a time when the teacher sits with one student while that student reads.

* **Writing conference**—a time when the teacher sits with one student or a small group of students to discuss writing problems, concerns,

intentions, or to answer questions about the writing.

* **L i t e r a r y letters**—letters written to teacher, parents, peers about a book being read.

* **Independent reading**—a time when students (and teacher) read on their own.

* **Independent writing**—a time when students (and teacher) write on their own.

* **Focus lessons**—specific lessons geared to the genre under study. These may be as general as the characteristics of a particular genre or as specific as character development, elaboration, voice, coherence.

* **Skills lessons**—specific lessons that hone in on skills such as capitalization, fragments, punctuation,

word attack, phonics, or even proper behaviors.

＊ Debriefings—short bursts of time at the conclusion of workshop meant to bring a sense of closure to the day's experience.

＊ **Share times**—allocated times for students to share with each other or with the teacher.

Each of these parts do not happen every day in the same way for every student or every teacher. Although the entire class may experience the minilesson, it is inevitable that minilessons will transpire when the teacher works one-on-one with a student or with a small group experiencing similar difficulty. Similarly, while some students write independently, others may be reading inde-

pendently. It is also
likely that when
most students are
reading, the teacher
may be sitting side-
by-side a student lis-
tening to that student
read; it is just as likely that when
most students are writing, the
teacher may be conducting a conference with a student about his or her
writing. The students may share
their writing or some aspect of their
reading in large group at the conclusion of workshop, or they may share
in small groups. Sometimes during
workshop, students read to each
other in small groups. In other
words, workshop ebbs and flows
with many productive activities
occurring simultaneously.

Chaos or Structured Complexity?

Teachers who place students' desks in rows with their desk front and center want sameness. They want all the students' papers to look alike; they want every student reading the same book at the same time. They are what I call "same pagers." If we think about that seriously for about twenty seconds (forget sound theory or pedagogy), just think about it sensibly, we realize how unrealistic that approach is. After all, we don't all look the same, nor dress, nor act, nor think, nor love, nor drive, nor emote, nor bear children, nor work, nor worship, ad infinitum, the same. Why would we want students to sit, to write, to read, to walk down the halls, often with their arms behind their backs, in the same way? Why would we teach them the same way at the same time or even expect them to hear everything or see everything in the same way? It's absurd really!

Obviously these "same pagers" view workshop as chaotic. "Good grief," they exclaim, "some kids are reading and some are writing. How do you keep track of everything?" Ah, therein lies the real problem—control. Teachers who want to control every action, every behavior of every student every moment will not cotton to workshop. But in the real world that is exactly how people work.

With cog jobs, jobs that demand assembly line training, on the wane, and with cognitive jobs, jobs that

13

demand initiative, rigor, self-discipline, choice, and thinking, on the rise, it behooves teachers to teach for the latter not the former. From that perspective workshop is not chaotic, rather it becomes sound training for a future calling for flexibility. Besides, if well-planned, well organized, and well-executed, workshop is not chaos. Rather as a well-oiled machine, workshop helps students develop what Michael Strong calls "the habit of thought." It allows for autonomy and frees teachers to truly teach.

Once, when I was observing a teacher involved in workshop, she looked at me and asked, "Why did it take me so long to teach like this? It's so wonderful." I looked around at her well-oiled machine: Three students were typing final drafts into their computers; some, already finished that writing project, were reading; one student was nose deep into two tomes, "Doing research," he muttered. Others were still writing, and three girls were sharing their writing, "...before we type it for good," they patiently explained. The one student nestled in the corner folding paper told us, "I'm planning my book. I want it to open up different 'cause what I wrote is pretty complicated."

So think of workshop as structured complexity—that is a single process called learning which is made up of interrelated parts. Things are not chancy; they are designed. Hence, the need for organization.

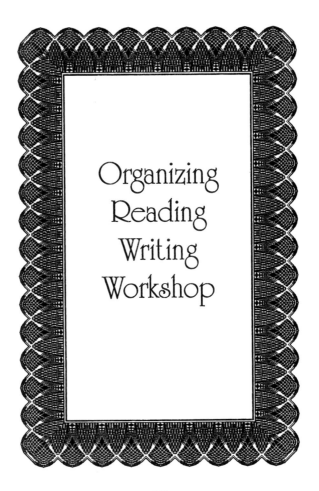

Organizing
Reading
Writing
Workshop

16

Before Initiating

Before starting workshop, divide students into groups and give each group a piece of colorful butcher paper. They divide the paper in half. On one side they brainstorm all the words they associate with the word *work*. On the other side, they brainstorm all the words they associate with the word *shop*. When they are finished, display the butcher paper, discuss words from each group. Invite generalizations. Students usually associate *work* with hard, an obligation, something you have to do; whereas *shop* generally suggests fun, going to the mall, making choices. When compounded, the students have a kid-friendly concrete notion of what you are about to introduce. Workshop is hard work, but fun, and it allows for choice.

Managing Time

Just as students have choices during workshop so, too, do teachers. One such choice is how to organize and manage the time. I offer five models. These are designed for six-week marking periods, but each may be adapted to the particular needs of any given schedule, time block, or group of students.

When beginning workshop, make one choice from among these models, explain everything to the students, and stick to that model for at least one marking period. If teacher and/or students are new to workshop, it takes a bit of time to move away from the prescriptive model and feel secure with the freedom of choice. But remember: it is through structured freedom and choice that students grow in their ability to shoulder responsibility and teachers grow in their professional life. (These models are not offered in any particular order.)

About Model I

Consider this model if workshop is familiar, if the students are eager, and if both are flexible. Model I alternates its emphasis on reading and on writing, although both are done every week in integrated ways. It also assumes students have had experience with writing and reading as processes, know the terminology, and are mature enough to work toward goal.

Model I

🔖 Minilesson and/ or Status-of-the-Class

🔖 Week 1—READING TIME—One-on one reading. Literary Letters: 1/3 of the class writes for teacher as audience; 1/3 writes for parent or trusted adult as audience; 1/3 writes for a peer as audience. Reading in the genre under study.

🔖 Week 2—WRITING TIME— Prewriting activities for four days. These may be writing in response to a book, poem, or essay, doing an activity such as blueprinting, trigger words, or hexagonal writing. (See Carroll & Wilson, *Acts of Teaching* for in-depth descriptions of possible prewriting activities.) On the fifth day, move students to the genre under study.

🔖 Week 3—READING TIME—One-on-one reading. Literary Letters: a different 1/3 of the class writes for teacher as audience; 1/3 writes for parent or trusted adult as audience; 1/3 writes for a peer as audience. Reading in the genre under study.

↶ Week 4—WRITING TIME—Writing—Ratiocination, reentering the paper, color coding it according to specific directions to make it better (See Carroll & Wilson, *Acts of Teaching* for instructions on ratiocination), Grammar within the Writing Process, Group Work, Conferences, and establishing the rubric for assessing the writing.

↶ Week 5—READING TIME—One-on one reading. Literary Letters: a different 1/3 of the class writes for teacher as audience; 1/3 writes for parent or trusted adult as audience; 1/3 writes for a peer as audience. Reading in the genre under study.

↪ Week 6—WRITING TIME—Together going over the rubric, Clocking, a collective way for students to proofread each other's papers, Editing, each student makes the final changes on his or her paper. Read-Around and/or Publishing. Literary letters and process compositions are filed in portfolios.

About Model II

Consider this model to give students optimum choice. This is an excellent model for workshop if teacher and students are able to juggle many apples in the air simultaneously, and if the students are self-disciplined. This is probably NOT the best model for beginners—teachers or students. Model II allows students much more freedom than do the other models. It demands of students self-regulation and the ability to set and meet their own goals.

Model II

Purpose

Six weeks work is determined by genre: narrative, essay, poetry, drama, letter or sub-genres such as short story, memoir, persuasive essay, ballad, a script for a school skit.

Students choose what they do each day via status of the class.
At the end of the six weeks students are expected to have kept up with, produced, or completed:

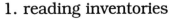

1. reading inventories
2. writing folders
3. literary letters
4. a paper which has been taken through the process.

(See Tracking Reading Writing Workshop beginning on page 43.)

Daily Format
↪ Minilesson
↪ Status-of-the-class
↪ Workshop time
↪ Closure/debriefing

About Model III

Consider this model as a first step, as a way to ease into workshop or if the students are a handful. This establishes a set structure and a time for direct teaching on Monday and Friday. The three days intervening days are available for some choice. Yet the groupings help the teacher maintain control. Model III presents a good way to begin workshop because the teacher directly teaches two days (and this is familiar to students) and then works specifically with a different but individual group the other three days. Thus, two groups are on their own each of those three days.

Model III

Monday	Tuesday	Wednesday	Thursday	Friday
Set Up Week; Whole Group instruction	GR. I Reading	GR. I Writing	GR. I Teacher	Closure Literary Letters; Testing; Review; Makeup; Whole Group Instruction
	GR. II Writing	GR. II Teacher	GR. II Reading	
	GR. III Teacher	GR. III Reading	GR. III Writing	

About Model IV

Consider imple-menting this model after implementing Model III as a way of gentling students into a more unstructured workshop environment. This model follows Model III because Monday and Friday remain constant and familiar to students, but Tuesday, Wednesday, and Thursday evolve into a more open format with more choice for students and teacher. After the minilesson, all the students read for a set time and then all the students write for a set time. After this model is in place for a time, students begin moving naturally from reading to writing and writing to reading, often reading some during the writing time or writing during the reading time. Notice, in this model, the teacher is able to work with individual students or small groups as needed three days a week.

Model IV

Monday	Tuesday	Wednesday	Thursday	Friday
Set Up Week; Whole Group instruction	Minilesson 10 minutes			Closure Literary Letters; Testing; Review; Makeup; Whole Group Instruction
	Reading 20 minutes			
	Writing 20 minutes			

About Model V (The Katherine Dowling Model)

Consider this model for primary or elementary classes or for self-contained classrooms. Model V is structured by the day, but clearly allows for choice and work-shop time after S.S.R. Additionally, each day, three to five students are chosen to read one-on-one for a specified time with the teacher during workshop. So from three to five students read one-on-one with the teacher on Monday, three to five on Tuesday, and so forth. How students are chosen is based on ability and time. Three struggling readers on one day may work, whereas five good readers could be taken on another day. Sometimes teachers like to mix the strugglers with the advanced readers to allow for pacing (and personal sanity!)

Model V

8:00 - 8:15	S.S.R.
8:15 - 9:50	Reading/Writing Workshop
9:50 - 10:00	Snack
10:00 - 10:25	Recess
10:25 - 11:15	Literature/ Writing
11:15 - 11:50	Music
11:50 - 12:30	Lunch
12:30 - 1:30	Mathematics
1:30 - 2:00	Physical Education
2:00 - 3:00	Recess/Centers Sharing/ Debriefing
3:00	Carpool

The Three Book Classroom

Once workshop is underway and running smoothly, introduce students to the concept of the three-book classroom. This extends reading choices to students and enables them to choose books that range in level and difficulty.

The First Book

This is the book students self-select for pleasure, for fun, for what Victor Nell calls "ludic" reading, that is paratelic or engaged in for its own sake. These are usually "fast" reads, books students love, books by authors they love, books they want to reread, series books, or books recommended by friends. They keep this book with them at all times and grab a read whenever they have spare time.

In this fast-moving world, few of us have long, leisurely times to read extensively. Rather we, too, if we are readers, grab ten minutes here, a few minutes there until we eventually finish our book. This is not a bad thing to model and talk about with kids. Too often students hear adults proclaim, "I don't have time to read," when they really mean, "I don't make time to read—even a little." Let students see the teacher grab a book when there is minute or two of free time. Never underestimate the power of modeling.

Remember: aside from the responsibility of entering this book in their reading inventory, students do no other assignment for this book. Let them learn that some reading can be for pure enjoyment.

The Second Book

This is a group-selected book from an approved list for small group reading. Students reading the same book gather together to read or to talk about what they have read. This is what literate people do. This is what people do who belong to reading clubs or study groups. Extending this into some sort of an assignment is the teacher's call. Some teachers, in addition to having students enter this book in their inventories, invite literary letters, entries into reading logs, reading journals, or reading notebooks, as a way to check comprehension. Others create interesting hands-on responses such as making bookmarks, folding a quincunx, creating pop-up books, flap or flip books on which students write about or out of the book: what they learned, connections, their favorite part, favorite character, and so forth. Doing something unique rewards the reader for reading, addresses different types of learners, provides a way to check comprehension; and, eventually as the reading increases, extends reading stamina. The power of the second book is the power of the peer.

The Third Book

This book, usually one of stellar literary merit, is teacher-selected from the basal or a language arts text; it is a book available in enough copies for each student. These are sometimes ancillary books provided by book companies through book adoptions, or books available through grant monies allocated for books.

Using this book with the entire class enables the teacher to conduct whole-group directed lessons, focus lessons, skill lessons on vocabulary, inference, theme, narrative elements, figurative language, and so forth. The goal, of course, is to deepen the love of reading and literature through a deeper understanding of technique and craft.

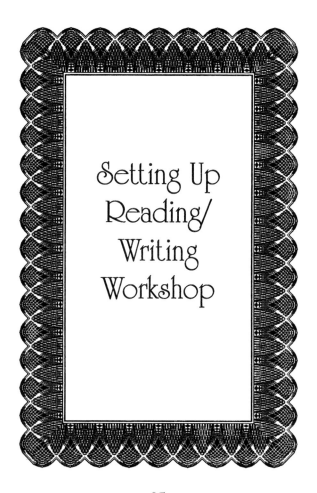

Setting Up
Reading/
Writing
Workshop

35

Crucial to the success of workshop is setting it up. There are two levels of setting up: the teacher's responsibilities and the students' responsibilities. Both share in the accountability of keeping the room in order, the materials neat, orderly, and in a mutually agreed upon relegated places.

The Teacher's Responsibilities

While workshop encourages individual choice, the teacher is the facilitator. Speaking metaphorically, the teacher is the map upon which the workshop is laid out. Set the tone for workshop by

◆ thinking ahead about students' needs during workshop and then discussing the room arrangement—what it can offer and how it is constrained—with the students. Things like: "Where shall we hold our reading/writing connections?" "Where shall we store all the materials we'll need for writing?" "Where would be the best place for one-on-one reading?" Do we need anything else?" help the sense of shared ownership. Teachers' responsibilities include:

◆ listening to what the students suggest;

◆ crafting interesting minilessons or microminilessons based on perceived student needs in both reading and writing;

◆ keeping minilessons to micro or mini and not extending the point into a full-blown class-period lesson;

◆ monitoring and adjusting constantly throughout workshop;

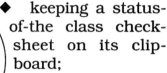

♦ keeping a status-of-the class check-sheet on its clip-board;

♦ obtaining a log book for keeping track of conferences;

♦ finding a rug or carpet squares upon which students can sit for reading and sharing;

♦ furnishing a comfortable or unique chair for the AUTHOR'S CHAIR. This chair becomes "sacred" as it is only used when an author (including the teacher) is sharing what he/she wrote;

♦ equipping the room with an IN BOX for papers ready to be read;

♦ equipping the room with a HOLDING TANK for reading tapes;

♦ equipping the room with a FIN-ISHED BOX for papers ready to be graded;

♦ providing needed materials.

Materials

Besides the obvious need for plenty of books to read in all genre, all lengths, all levels of difficulty, contemporary and classic, paperback and hard back, and plenty of paper in all colors, weights, and sizes on which to write, a good workshop needs

◆ magazines and journals and other reading materials such as bulletins, posters, advertisements, memos, letters, poetry books, reference books—plenty of dictionaries (a variety), all manner of synonym books, idiom books, word books, bad spellers' dictionaries, grammar/writers' reference books, handbooks, and reading material that offers models for writing;

◆ index cards, post-its®, highlighter tape, butcher paper;

♦ markers, crayons, highlighters, gel pens, all kinds of pencils and pens;

♦ hole punchers, staplers, plenty of paper clips, rubber bands, chicken rings, and brads;

♦ scissors, rulers, yarn, ribbon, twine;

♦ stamps and stickers of all kinds, glue and glue sticks, rubber cement, aluminum foil, paper coffee filters, paper plates, paper napkins thick enough to write on, paper bags all sizes, plastic baggies;

♦ erasers and white out;

♦ computers and typewriters;

♦ plastic crates for filing students folders;

♦ file folders, two per student as a place to keep reading and writing work in progress.

The Students' Responsibilities

While teachers facilitate workshop, students participate actively in its design and execution. Speaking metaphorically, if the teacher is map upon which the workshop is laid out, students are the travelers. Students help the success of the workshop by:

◆ honoring individual choice, space, and time

◆ not interrupting;

◆ working to establish guidelines that maximize learning for themselves and others in the class;

◆ reading and writing with verve and zest;

◆ using the workshop time wisely;

◆ knowing where materials are;

◆ reading or writing if there is extra

◆ storing all writing—writing as responses to reading as well as all writing in process—literary letters, prewriting, drafts, ideas, leads, notes from minilessons—in file folders at the proper preordained place;

◆ listening to those who are sharing;

◆ giving thoughtful feedback.

Tracking
Reading/
Writing
Workshop

This part of work-shop must be clear to all involved because assessment hinges upon it. Records must be kept in tidy, organized and productive ways, and they should be kept in specific and consistent places in the classroom. Obviously, since this is reading/writing work-shop, records for both reading and writing must be kept by both the students and the teacher.

For students, record keeping trains them to take responsibility for their learning. They keep track of their reading and writing in order to show evidence that what the teacher is teaching, they are learning. Students generally like this task—it empowers them, generates a feeling of ownership, and makes them truly feel part of the process.

For teachers, there are two major objectives in keeping records of any kind to be used for future assessment: simplicity and accuracy.

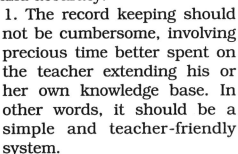

1. The record keeping should not be cumbersome, involving precious time better spent on the teacher extending his or her own knowledge base. In other words, it should be a simple and teacher-friendly system.

2. The system must reflect as accurately as possible the true work, level, progress, process, and success or lack of success of each student.

Easy to say—not so easy to accomplish, yet to accomplish these two objectives frees the teacher to study, read, and bring spontaneity and

 excitement to the lesson. When teachers bog down in pyramids of paperwork, morale and energy and students suffer.

Student Kept Reading Records

Reading Inventories

Students keep two reading inventories. One chronicles the genres read in the three-book classroom—the self-sponsored reading, the small group reading, and the teacher selected, large group reading. The other reflects the amount of reading the student has done. Taken together they provide both the student and the teacher a clear picture of the student's reading fluency as well as the breadth of choice made and the genres to which the student has been exposed. The idea is that while all readers have genres to which they gravitate, school is the time to taste other types.

Credit, something like a 90/10 split, should be given for the amount read (90%) and for variety attempted (10%). For example: If a student reads three science fiction novels, one essay, and a biography as self-sponsored reading, an adventure novel or story in small group, and several pieces of nonfiction with the class, that student would get high marks for both fluency and for diversity.

On the other hand, if a student reads nothing but romances for ludic reading, chooses to be in the small group that reads a romance, and only does the nonfiction with the teacher, that student may do well for fluency but not for diversity.

To record both, the student keeps the *Genre Reading Inventory* (See p. 120) which enables the checking off of the various types of genre undertaken weekly as well as the *Reading Inventory Goal Setting Sheet* (See p. 125) which enables the weekly setting of pages as a goal for fluency. (Samples of both of these inventories may be found on pages 120 and 125.) These inventories are kept in the individual student's Reading Folder.

Reading Folders

These are file folders in which the students keep their reading inventories. These folders are kept in the room in an inexpensive but durable plastic filing carton. (One for each

class in middle and
high school or in
cases of departmen-
talization in the
lower grades.) Each
student is responsi-
ble for filing his or her
folder at the end of class and retrieving it at the beginning of class.
Students also keep their Reading
Memory Quires in this folder.

Reading Memory Quires
These are simply eight-page books
(See p. 127) that can be quickly
made out of loose leaf paper or plain
photocopy paper. Students keep one
of these handy as they read in order
to jot down something worth remem-
bering: an unusual word, something
that strikes them, an important bit
of information, something that con-
fuses them, some question that arises, or general notes.

Student Kept Writing Records

Writing Inventories

Just as students follow the yellow brick road of their reading, so, too, must they follow what happens as they make choices about their writing. Writing inventories, like the reading inventories, come in two types.

Writing Performance Profile is a type of self-assessment that enables students to describe not only the processes but the progress of their writing. The writing performance profile looks for items as shown in the appendix (See p. 123). Students' comments on each item are usually kept as short narrative notes, for example, "I spent twenty minutes rewriting today."

When writers consider the time spent on task, they need to interpret that time in terms of effort. When considering effort, students need to assess what was accomplished. The effectiveness of the writing relates directly to the quality of the work done.

The Structure/Mechanics Writing Inventory (See p. 124), as its name suggests, reinforces structure and mechanics. Here the student checks for the FORM of the genre—beginning, middle, end for narrative—introduction, body, conclusion for an essay, for example, and for the mechanics. Commas, fragments, capitals, would be checked on this inventory.

Students check off the various modes and purposes they undertake in their writing—under the umbrella of FICTION/NON-FICTION followed first by the major structures such as narrative then followed by the substructures such as memoir or flash fiction. Not only does this encourage students to poke around into other genres, but it has a way of helping students make correct choices when mixing genres. For example, a student may be working on narrative but realize a big chunk of the piece is descriptive or a student may choose to insert a line or two of poetry in the middle of a story. The student may do this by having a character quote from a poem to make a point. Then the student is able to check off fiction, narrative, descriptive, poetry on the Writing Inventory.

Writing Folders

These are folders in which the students keep their writing inventories. These folders are kept in the room in an inexpensive but durable plastic filing carton. (One carton for each class in middle and high school or in cases of departmentalization in the lower grades.) Each student assumes the responsibility for filing his or her folder at the end of class and retrieving it at the beginning of class. Students also keep their Literary Letters in this folder, ideas for future writing, quotations they love, snippets from pieces of literature which they might use for literary borrowing, text innovation, work in progress, prewritings, and anything else they might want to save to help them become better and better writers.

Literary Letters

These foster literacy because they encourage students to emulate in writing what literate people think and say when they talk about what they read. For example, it would not be unusual for a friend to ask, "Hi Sara, have you read ____?" If Sara answers in the affirmative, it would be quite unusual for the next question to be, "Can you name the major characters?" or "What is the theme of the book?" or "Give me one place where you inferred." Instead, literate people talk INTO and UP TO the books they read, using their reading skills to support and underpin what they are discussing. That is the purpose of the *Literary Letter*, to provide a place for literacy to happen, for students to talk INTO and UP TO the books they read, using their skills and vocabulary to make their points.

Many skills are reinforced with the literary letter. First, the student must address the letter to a specific audience: teacher, parent/ trusted adult, or peer. That sense of audience carries with it two side effects: voice and tone. No student, for example, uses the same voice and tone for a teacher or for a friend.

Second, the writer must use the structure of the letter. The by-product here is that structure becomes more and more internalized. Third, the literary letter is NOT a retelling of what was read but rather takes an angle and elaborates upon it. For example, a student would not retell the plot of Kate DiCamillo's *Because of Winn-Dixie* in a literary letter,

 rather, after reading Chapter One, the three literary letters might look like this:

To the teacher:

September 25, 200_

Dear Ms. Smithye,

I just finished the first chapter of Kate Di Camillo's Because of Winn-Dixie and I wanted to thank you for recommending that book to me. How did you know I loved dogs? I would have done exactly what Opal did. I would have tried to save some poor old stray who wandered into a grocery store probably because he was hungry. And, I would have talked to him just the way Opal did, "Come on. Let's see what the preacher [her Daddy] has to say about you." I can hardly wait to read the next chapter. I

think her Daddy will let
her keep Winn-Dixie. I
wonder if she`ll call
him both names or just
Winn like Win for
Winner!

Your student,
Justina

P.S. What else has Kate Di Camillo written? I want to read everything she writes.

To the parent:

September 25, 200_

Dear Mom and Dad,

OK, you are always ragging me to read, read, read, Well, you can quit picking on me about that. I just found the best book! Ms. Smithye told me about it. (I guess she knows I love dogs.) India Opal Buloni, the heroine, is just like me. She's creative and thinks quick on her feet. Because she is so smart she saves a dog from going to the pound. She names the dog Winn-Dixie, just like the grocery store. I don't want to give the story away, but I can tell you that I'm going to read, read, read it every chance I have. I just know that dog will figure somehow into the book, probably save somebody, maybe even Opal.

Your daughter,
Justina

P.S. Could you buy me this book?

P.S.S. I think it's on Amazon.

To a peer:
September 25, 200_

Dear Luis,

   Remember when we talked about wanting to get a dog? Well, I`m reading a book Ms. Smithye told me about. It`s all about how this girl with a really funny name, India Opal Buloni (like the lunch meat! Ha Ha) gets a dog in the grocery store! You wouldn`t believe what she names it. Guess. Winn-Dixie. Yep! Just like the grocery store, so the dog has a funny name too. And get this, the dog smiles. Gosh! I'd love to find a smiling dog in a grocery store. I`d give it a cool name *too.*

Your friend in dogs,
Justina

P.S. The name of the book
is Because of Winn-Dixie.

By reading these literary letters, it is obvious that Justina has read the first chapter and understands the character's motivation, is able to incorporate a quote from the book, and uses different registers of language to match the appropriate audience while retaining her authentic voice. As Justina gets more into the book, her letters become longer (there is more to munch on) and she is able to incorporate more devices she notices Di Camillo using. In one literary letter, she noted: *"That Kate Di Camillo is some*

61

author. She even had Sweetie
Pie making a mistake in
grammar. She says `I brung
tape, too!` That tells me
something about Sweetie
Pie."

The plus of literary letters is that they also provide an authentic way to have students respond to what they are reading through their writing in a comfortable and familiar genre. Responding to literature offers a natural way into writing in addition to the *Writing Process*.

The Writing Process

Evidence of the writing process belongs in the Student's Writing Folder. All the pre-writing, drafting, ratiocinating, revising, proofreading, clocking, the analytic scale, and ultimately the published piece should find its home in each student's writ-

ing folder. At the con-
clusion of a marking
period or semester,
the students read
through all the work
in their folders and
choose their best writ-
ing to be dated and placed in their
Writing Portfolios.

Writing Portfolios

The Writing Portfolio acts as an
ongoing place for students to store
examples of selected pieces of writing. Unlike the writing folder, which
serves as a storage file for all writing,
portfolios are receptacles of what
students, teachers, peers, and parents deem the best writing.
Portfolios should be like the student,
unique. No two portfolios should be
the same.

I have developed the *Portfolio
Profile of Student Capabilities (PPSC).*

This model empha-sizes student auton-omy and student ability to engage in self-assessment. The *PPSC* invites stu-dents and teachers to look at the students' capabilities. Skills, genre, tests happen else-where. This is the place to show off the best very much the way artists or designers create a portfolio of their best work. (See p. 128 for more on the *PPSC*. Also check *Acts of Teaching*.)

Teacher Kept
Reading Records

*Teacher's Reading
File Folders*

In addition to the student-kept files, teachers need a file with a reading folder for each student. In that folder, teachers keep copies of literary letters—sent and received as evidence of reading. These letters may be assessed in the traditional way or they may be credited toward meeting the criteria of three letters. That would be the teacher's call. (See section on assessment.)

Here teachers also keep photocopies of students' inventories which they check to see if students met their goals and if they challenged themselves to dabble in a variety of genre. The best and easiest way to do this is to photocopy the literary letters and inventories weekly and use post-its® to keep anecdotal notes about progress, concerns, surprises, achievements, problems, vocabulary, or whatever emerges from the letters and inventories. Also, all reading tests are kept in this file folder.

Minilessons

Short lessons that arise from the reading or lessons relate to reading skills are kept by the teacher in a lesson plan booklet of some sort, a small index file on the desk, or in a separate file folder. These may be color coded by level of difficulty and should be within easy reach for the perceived teachable moment as well as a ready reference to use before students engage in workshop.

Teachers refer to these minilessons when checking evidence of the lesson learned in the students' work.

Spontaneous minilessons or microminies, that arise naturally during a class or a conference, may be jotted down on loose leaf paper, index cards or post-its® to be saved for future reference.

One-on-One Reading Records

When teachers read one-on-one with students, they keep notes on what happens during that time. This is perhaps the most important time shared between teacher and student, a time when teachers check comprehension, skills, and fluency. The teacher keeps a checklist for each student, one that reserves a place to check skills such as inference, predicting, etc. as initial attempts, applications, and mastery as well as a place for commentary and clarification. (See p. 121 for an example of this type of record.)

Reading Tapes

Some teachers like to use reading tapes as a way to facilitate independent reading by students as well as a way to record their oral reading. The best and easiest way to do this is to invite students to read one page of their self-sponsored book, one page of their group book, and one page of the teacher-selected book on tape. By hearing these three pages of differing difficulty, the teacher has an oral record of degree of mastery for each student, one the teacher may refer to when evaluating or when discussing the student's progress with parents.

Each student begins by giving his or her name and the title and page of each selection just before reading from it. This detail develops the habit of giving attribution. When the taping has been completed, another student may begin taping. All tapes should be placed in some holding tank (See p. 118) until the teacher can get to them. Notes taken while listening to the tapes may be included with the one-on-one records.

Teacher Kept Writing Records

Teacher's Writing File Folders

Teachers need a writing file folder for each student. Photocopies of writing done as evidence of the writing process, additional self-sponsored writing, and the analytic scale should be stored in these folders. Additionally, any notes the teacher makes during conference or any observations made as the students work should find its way into the writing file folder.

The Analytic Scale

This assessment tool is crucial to evaluating the writing process of students. The teacher and students develop a scoring rubric together. They determine what the teacher has taught and what the students should have learned. These things should show up in the students' writing. Based on the Diederich scale, these scales are geared to help the student achieve success by knowing beforehand what is expected. Each student receives a scale after the class has brainstormed: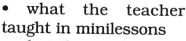

• what the teacher taught in minilessons

• what the teacher taught in direct teaching.

After the brainstorming, the teacher weights each item and creates the scale. Students are given copies of these scales before they enter into clocking. (Clocking is a technique that enables peer proofreading and better editing.) After clocking, each student has still another go at making his or her paper better.

Keeping these rubrics after the writing process has been completed is worthwhile because the analytic scale is both a numerical evaluation and an anecdotal one. As it also reserves a place for commentary, it is an invaluable documentation of each student's work. Additionally, the analytic scale can be built to accommodate the writing process as well as the skills and concepts taught during minilessons and direct teaching. (See pgs. 132-133 for sample analytic scales.)

Teacher Kept Reading/Writing Records

Status-of-the-Class

This method of keeping track on a daily basis comes from Nanci Atwell. In her book *In the Middle*, she defines status-of-the-class as "a grid listing the names of all the students in a class down the left-hand margin, with a box for each day of the week next to each name" (Atwell 73). This record keeping system is quick, efficient, and gives a thumbnail sketch of where every student is every day. (See p. 122 for a sample.)

These three ways to track students provide a dynamic and effective systematic daily documentation of each students' reading and writing. They are eminently "do-able" and provide a valid and systematic reconstruction of work done each day, each week, each marking period.

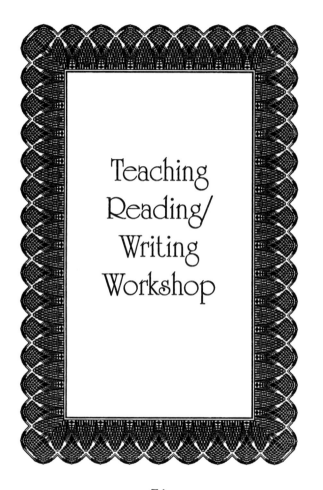

Teaching
Reading/
Writing
Workshop

Teaching within the context of workshop is challenging yet joyful. Because the teacher works so often and so intensely most of the time with individual students, there is a contagious energy in the room. Besides, such individualized instruction permits learning to occur most specifically and most noticeably. Students easily see their writing improve with the specificity of instruction and immediate application and they realize that their reading improves as they receive direct help on their individual stumbling blocks.

In both reading and writing, the daily encouragement and the variety of choice creates a natural learning environment—what Frank Smith in his *The Book of Learning and Forgetting* calls "the classic view of learning and forgetting." He names this manner of learning *classic* because "it is archetypal, universal, deeply rooted, and uncontaminated." He holds that "we learn from people around us with whom we identify" (Smith 3). That is exactly what happens in workshop. Students join a literacy club where they come together under the guidance and facilitation of a teacher who loves reading, writing, thinking, and sharing—then together all become learners.

In any given school or district, there is a curriculum or some type of master framework that sets out the objectives students are expected to achieve as they journey through their education. Texas has the TEKS (Texas Essential Knowledge and

Skills) and the state mandated test TAKS (Texas Assessment of Knowledge and Skills). These expectations in the field of English Language Arts encompass concepts such as word identification, vocabulary, comprehension; or, phrased more specifically, skills such as idioms, multi-meaning words, analogies, figurative language, roots, prefixes, affixes, denotation, connotation, main ideas and supporting details, paraphrases and summaries to name just a few. These are what good ELA teachers teach, and the great teachers, knowing their learning theory and brain research, manage to teach these concepts and skills in a meaningful context. Workshop provides just that context.

Minilessons and Micro-minilessons

These spurts of teaching are short, powerful bits that fit exactly into what the student needs to be successful during that phase of workshop, or, as in the case of the micro-minilesson, what the student needs at that moment. For example, if students are beginning a new paper—whatever the genre—a minilesson on leads might be appropriate—not one on conclusions. If the genre under study is the persuasive essay, then a micro-minilesson on its structure would be apt. If the teacher, while monitoring, sees that comma splices are a problem for some students, such a skills lesson would help those students, especially since they could make application in their writing immediately. There are many books worth consulting on mini-lessons. (See the Suggested Sources with annotations on pages 101 - 115.)

Direct Teaching

A misconception about workshop that often arises is that teachers no longer teach and that students do whatever they want. *Au contraire.* Those who hold this misconception are misinformed. Direct teaching has its place in workshop. Indeed, Models III, IV, and V carve out entire days or hunks of time for just such teaching. Or, in so flexible a schedule as workshop, would it not be possible to stop any time the teacher perceives the need in order to do some direct instruction? Direct teaching is usually done with the entire class to introduce, motivate, troubleshoot, solve a widespread problem or dilemma, attack a rampant skill deficiency, or conclude a lesson.

As for students doing whatever they want, that also is misconstrued. True, students have some latitude of choice, but they also have deadlines, objectives, purposes, and responsibilities to meet those conditions set by the teacher.

Small Group Lessons

Classes, no matter how well screened, even if all students are labeled "Gifted," are never perfectly homogeneous. (Some are saying at this point, "That would be a little bit of heaven." Some are saying, "Tracking never worked anyway.") So it is likely in any given class, at various points in the reading or the writing process, the teacher might notice a small group suffering over the same or similar problems. For example, in writing, especially when beginning a new genre, pockets of students may become agitated by writers' block. Because of workshop, the teacher is able to gather those students together and nudge them into thinking in a new key (to borrow Susanne K. Langer's term). They might together do a quicklist, jot down holidays, read or look at picture books, comb through a newspaper, or simply talk. Any or all of these can unblock the anxious writer.

Another scenario might go like this. During status-of-the-class the teacher notices that some students apparently are having trouble finding a book to read. The teacher rounds them up. They talk informally about ways to choose a book: by looking at its cover to determine if it holds any appeal (which goes against the age-old axiom, "Don't judge a book by its cover."), by reading the back cover and the flaps, by trying out five or ten pages, by asking a friend, the teacher, the librarian for a recommendation, by reading the lists of winning books, by choosing a book by a recognized or loved author. Since this may not be the sticking point for all the students, a small group discussion might just do the trick for those who are stuck.

One-minute Conferences

Oh, those one-minute conferences work wonderfully in workshop. The teacher sits in a chair with wheels and simply rolls around the room from student to student from small group to small group making suggestions, nudging, recommending, listening, reading, proposing, counseling, advising, hinting, inferring, and, of course, teaching all the time. NCTE once ran this *bon mot* in one of its publications, "A one-minute conference is often worth all the red marginalia."

Incidental Teaching

Incidental in this context is not meant as unimportant but rather adscititious. Thus an extrinsic need may arise in a moment for a particular student, and the teacher takes the time to do a bit of incidental teaching. Incidental teaching is often fundamental; something a student may not want to ask in front of peers because he or she may feel everyone knows the answer, or something that simply presents itself while the student is writing. It may go something like this:

"Mr. W., do you have a second?"

"Sure, Christina, what do you need?"

"Does a comma go here," Christina asks pointing to a place on her paper.

"Yes, Christina, because we always put a comma when we are directly addressing someone.

Done. The incidental lesson is over.

The context may just as easily happen while a student is reading.

"Miss Z., I'm reading *Esparanza Rising*. Esparanza is the girl's name. What does it mean in English?"

"That's a wonderful question, Cheryl, because authors choose the names of characters with great care. Sometimes the name gives us insight into the character. Esparanza means hope. See how that might figure into the novel."

Again done. That's it. Nothing beaten to death. No diatribe on the significance of names, no harangue on symbolism, no quoting Romeo and Juliet, "What's in a name? That which we call a rose//By any other name would smell as sweet." Just the delivery of a quick incidental lesson.

The difference between the micro-minilesson and the incidental lesson lies in the source. The former rises up out of something observed by the teacher; the latter comes from a need voiced by a student.

Assessing
Reading/
Writing
Workshop

Workshop allows for comprehensive assessment of students' reading and writing abilities. In assessment, though, it is important to distinguish among the various ways to go about the act of evaluating. But just as classes are filled with disparate students coming from disparate backgrounds with disparate needs and disparate skills, so, too, assessment must take on variety in order to obtain a clear picture of the total student.

Assessing in only one way is like looking at a painting with a drop cloth covering part of it. No one would judge a painting without seeing it in its entirety. So, too, with assessing the ability of students in reading and writing. For instance, to only check their ability to word call when reading is to short shrift comprehension. To only check mechanics in writing is to short shrift the content. In order to get a total picture of each student in workshop, in order to evaluate each student thoroughly, teachers *judge, describe, measure, analyze, score,* and *grade.*

Judgment

Everything that happens in a classroom is fair game for *judgment.* The task is to make judgments reliable, not idiosyncratic or biased. Since total objectivity is impossible—we are, after all, human—any judgment should be supported by evidence, by documentation that may be anecdotal, empirical, and/or scientific.

Example: *Today Daniel wrote the entire work-*

shop time. He didn't disturb any-one and showed me a literary letter to his friend Roel. I loved what he said, "Roel will like this letter because it is about my dog. He has a chow chow dog with a black tongue." I think reading Shiloh made a difference for him. It seems to be the first book he really became engaged in. I must find more dog books for him. I think I'll suggest _Stone Fox_ next.

Description

When conferencing with a student in reading or writing, the teacher keeps general notes on the strategies the student uses, growth, process, attitude, performance, risk taking, skills used, skills in flux, skills not yet internalized, level of engagement, and the degree of joy with which the student approaches the subject.

Example: Tashia worked hard in her group today, but I was really impressed with her word attack skills when we sat one-on-one. Up until today she would simply not try a word she didn't know; but today was different. She worked at sounding out the initial sounds for words she didn't know and listened when I gave her clues. I am glad to see she is beginning to take risks in her reading.

Measurement

Using an analytic scale as a measurement device enables teachers to assess what they have taught. Employed over a period of time and stored as documentation, the analytic scale charts the student's progress. Further, scales enable students to focus their reading and writing on the descriptors (what has been taught, what is expected) in order to see for themselves what they can do, what they still have to work on, and what they cannot yet do.

Example: *Tony used the same old tired lead for his first two papers—a version of "One dark and stormy night." On this last paper, though, he received high marks for his lead. It really did* hook the reader, improved his paper, and improved his grade. He went from a 75% to an 84%--a nine point jump to be proud of.

Analysis

While *description* captures the general observations made about specifics, e.g. *"Al shows marked improvement in his word attack skills,"* *analysis* explicitly details the specifics, e.g. *"Al has conquered the blends and diphthongs and now is much better at reading words that contain them. Thus, his reading aloud has improved."*

What *analysis* encourages is a focus on specific skills as delineated by state, district, grade-level objectives. This "breaking apart" of skills allows for in-depth, substantive evaluation and gives specificity to the process of assessing.

Example: *Margaret is not conquering the prefixes as outlined in our TEKS Objectives. She writes them fine but does not test well on them.*

Scoring

Perhaps the most popular scoring procedure, primarily because of state mandated tests, is *holistic scoring*. This procedure sorts and ranks writing. Usually *holistic scoring* lists features such as content, voice, mechanics, process (or whatever was taught or is expected) and then ranks each paper high/high (4), high/low (3), low/high (2), or low/low (1). This type of scoring is usually done by two parties (and a third if necessary). It is quick, efficient, and if the scorers are well trained, valid and reliable. Teachers adapt this for workshop by identifying the qualities they expect in a paper or those they have taught. They score the students' papers accordingly.

Students profit from scored papers because they immediately see their ranking. If they received a 4, they must work to maintain that score, a 3 says, "work a little harder," a 2 is minimal, and a 1 tells the student to "get busy."

Example: *Fourteen of my 24 students scored a 2 on our benchmark test in writing, six scored a 3, seven made a four and one was absent.*

Grading

The traditional system of grading—either numerically or by letter grades—is one of the most pervasive practices in American education—and, ask any teacher, one of the most difficult. Summing up a corpus of work into one number or one letter is problematic. How do teachers account for effort or risk? What do teachers do about grading the brilliant but lazy student? What about the hard working but slow student? What of all the nuances that constitute the work of any given student? The best way around this dilemma is to grade everything. Grade:

- prewriting
- reader response
- choice of books
- making connections between and

 among books and to life
- skills
- application of minilessons, micro-minilessons, and direct lessons
- oral reading
- oral sharing
- one-on-one reading
- independent reading
- achievement of goals
- fulfilling contract of status-of-the-class
- drafting
- revising
- reformulating
- sentence combining
- ratiocination
- spelling
- compositional risk taking
- voice
- reading with verve
- fluency in reading

- fluency in writing
- specificity in writing
- comprehension
- inference
- title
- attribution
- structure
- incorporating quotations
- leads
- conclusions
- organization
- internal coherence
- external coherence
- clarity
- tone
- purpose
- important ideas
- supporting ideas
- figurative language
- capitals
- punctuation
- legibility
- publishing

- group work
- genre
- clocking
- conferencing
- vocabulary
- paragraphing
- sentence structure
- sentence variety
- dialogue
- bibliography
- multi-genre
- summarizing
- literary forms
- prefixes and affixes
- idioms
- word play
- cause/effect
- comparison/contrast
- thesis/antithesis
- tests
- responses to books, poems, essays, art, music
- predictions

- questions of higher order
- discussions
- setting
- theme
- depth in writing
- breadth in reading
- noting author's purpose

In short, when students ask, "Are you gonna' grade this?" The response is "I grade everything." In workshop there is no limit to what can be graded—just be certain the students are aware of what will and will not be graded. Class tests receive grades. Questions are weighted according to difficulty and the system that is used is shared with students.

Checklists

While superficial, checklists are quick ways to ascertain if certain criteria were met or if all requirements were met. These are best used *before* the final grade is given. *Clocking* uses a checklist as part of the proofreading/editing cycle of writing. (See p. 131 for example.)

Self-Evaluations

In workshop students are encouraged to constantly and consistently self-evaluate. In a formal system of self-evaluation, the students evaluate their own progress, usually in writing or in a conference with the teacher. This self-assessment is taken into consideration by the teacher when making any type of final evaluation. (An example of one type of self-evaluation log may be found in the Appendix, p. 129.)

Suggested
Sources

As a primer for implementing reading/writing workshop, we offer books for starting a professional library, videos that show how the pros go about workshop, and suggested books that extend the information in this short primer.

Videos

Calkins, Lucy McCormick, Shelley Harwayne, and Alex Mitchell. *The Writing Workshop Video: A World of Difference.* #08448. Heinemann, 1987.

> A classic. This video K-8 shows how a particular teacher's style impacts workshop. (40 minutes)

Daniels, Harvey. *Looking into Literature Circles.* AV-0336. Stenhouse, 2001.

> If you want to incorporate literature circles into workshop, Daniels tape is brief but helpful. He points out key organizing structures,

response logs, role sheets, and sticky notes. (15 minutes)

Dorn, Linda J. *Organizing for Literacy.* AV-0312. Stenhouse, 1999. (80 minutes)

While not specifically about workshop, these four tapes are perfect for young or inexperienced teachers who are teaching grades K-3. Tape 1 deals with organizing the classroom; tape 2 addresses learning about reading; tape 3 looks at writing; tape 4 concentrates on words.

Fletcher, Ralph and JoAnn Portalupi. *When Students Write.* AV-0334. Stenhouse, 2001. (120 minutes)

This video shows master teachers putting the ideas of workshop into practice with students. The four tapes in this series cover choice, creating a risk-taking environment, skills and craft, the writing process, literature, and more.

Harvey, Stephanie and Anne Goudvis. *Strategy Instruction in Action.* AV-0335. Stenhouse, 2001. (120 minutes)

A look at creating a culture of thinking, modeling questions in a reading workshop, reading and understanding nonfiction, and using strategies to enhance book club discussions. Excellent.

Hindley, Joanne. *Inside Reading and Writing Workshops.* AV-0071. Stenhouse, 1998. (80 minutes)

These four tapes show reading and writing workshop operating in a third-grade classroom. The video highlights reading and writing minilessons, resources, strategies, and challenges surrounding workshop.

Books

Allen, Janet and Kyle Gonzalez. *There's Room for Me Here: Literacy Workshop in the Middle School.* Stenhouse, 1998.

This book features Kyle Gonzalez's classroom—how she sets it up, offers intervention, and supports struggling students.

Anderson, Carl. *How's it Going? A Practical Guide to Conferring with Student Writers.* Portsmouth, NH: Heinemann, 2000.

If you need help on conferencing, here's your book.

Atwell, Nanci. *In the Middle: New Understandings about Writing, Reading, and Learning.* (2nd edition). Portsmouth, NH: Heinemann, 1998.
> Great book for the middle school teacher.

Bailey, LaWanda. *Miss Myrtle Frag, the Grammar Nag.* Spring, TX: Absey & Co., 2000.
> Perfect grammar vignettes to use in workshop.

Bridges, Lois. *Writing as a Way of Knowing.* Stenhouse, 1997.
> Another guide into workshop.

Brock, Paula. *Nudges.* Spring, TX: Absey & Co., 2002.
> Brock gives ideas for vocabulary and writing.

Bullock, Richard (ed). *Why Workshop? Changing Course in 7-12 English.* Stenhouse, 1998.
> The essays in this book offer advice on

overviews, elements, philosophy, and the methods of workshop.

Burke, Jim. *Reading Reminders: Tools, Tips, and Techniques.* Portsmouth, NH: Heinemann, 2000.

Burke shares 100 of the best techniques of teaching reading.

_____. *The English Teacher's Companion: A Complete guide to Classroom, Curriculum, and the Profession.* Urbana, IL: NCTE, 1999.

Highly accessible and easy to use, this book is geared for grades K-College.

Buss, Kathleen and Lee Karnowski. *Reading and Writing Nonfiction Genres.* Newark, DE: International Reading Association, 2002.

Appropriate for grades two through six, this book explores the four main genre of nonfiction.

Calkins, Lucy McCormick. *The Art of Teaching Writing.* Portsmouth, NH:

106

Heinemann, 1994. (new edition)

A classic on the writing workshop.

Carroll, Joyce Armstrong and Edward E. Wilson. *Acts of Teaching: How to Teach Writing.* Englewood, CO: Teachers' Ideas Press/Libraries Unlimited, 1993.

This book provides a comprehensive look at writing as a process. Pedagogy and theory blend to make this a must for every teacher of writing.

Carroll, Joyce Armstrong. *Dr. JAC's Guide to Writing with Depth.* Absey and Co., 2002.

Depth features strategies for getting depth into writing as well as focus, organization, and voice. Models come from childrens', young adult, classic, and contemporary literature with suggestions for easy application. A resource for every writer and teacher of writing.

_____. *The Best of Dr. JAC.* Spring, TX: Absey & Co., 1998.

A source for reading/writing connections. Lessons and extensions are time and teacher tested.

Cary, Stephen. *Second Language Learners.* Stenhouse, 1997.

Cary helps K-6 teachers and administrators bring second language learners to proficiency. There are plenty of visuals and student samples as supporting evidence and plenty of teacher-tested ideas.

Charbula, Barbara. *Before the Test.* Spring, TX: Absey & Co., 2002.

In compelling narrative style, Charbula tells how she taught her students and how they excelled on the state-mandated test. Great model.

Ericson, Bonnie (ed.). *Teaching Reading in High School English Classes.* Urbana, IL: NCTE, 2001.

This book presents a collection of essays that offer practical teaching ideas for helping students increase vocabulary and comprehension grades 7-12.

Fletcher, Ralph and JoAnn Portalupi. *Writing Workshop: The Essential Guide.* Portsmouth, NH: Heinemann, 2001.

This guide delivers what it promises by covering time, space, goals, skills, assessment, troubleshooting, and a vast, practical appendix of practical forms.

_____. *Craft Lessons: Teaching Writing K-8.* Stenhouse, 1998.
Practical and easy to read. Presents 78 lessons.

_____. *Nonfiction Craft Lessons: Teaching Information Writing K-8.* Stenhouse 2001.
Ditto above—only in this book there are 80 lessons.

Fountas, Irene C. and Gay Su Pinnell. *Guiding Readers and Writers Grades 3-6.* Portsmouth, NH: Heinemann, 2001.
As the cover says, "Teaching Comprehension, Genre, and Content Literacy." This book also features 1000 leveled books.

Gere, Anne Ruggles and Peter Shaheen (eds.) *Making American Literatures in High School and College.* Urbana, IL: 2001.
This book is filled with lively and compelling teaching ideas for grades 8-college.

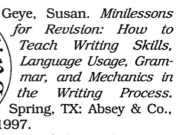

Geye, Susan. *Minilessons for Revision: How to Teach Writing Skills, Language Usage, Grammar, and Mechanics in the Writing Process.* Spring, TX: Absey & Co., 1997.

Geye offers a series of thirty-eight mini-lessons that show teachers how to maximize teaching while minimizing time.

Gunnery, Sylvia. *Just Write! Ten Practical Workshops for Successful Student Writing.* Stenhouse, 1998.

This book addresses writers 7-12 and ways they can do workshop.

Harvey, Stephanie and Anne Goudvis. *Strategies That Work: Teaching Comprehension to Enhance Understanding.* Stenhouse, 2000.

The authors answer the question: What's after decoding?

Jackson, Norma R. and Paula L. Pillow. *The Reading-Writing Workshop: Getting Started.* NY: Scholastic, 1992.

An easy guide to starting workshop.

Lane, Barry and Gretchen Bernabei. *Why We Must Run with Scissors: Voice Lessons in Persuasive Writing.* Shoreham, VT: Discover Writing Press, 2001.
Eighty-two practical lessons for grades 3-12

Marshall, Jodi Crum. *Are They Really Reading? Expanding SSR in the Middle Grades.* Stenhouse, 2002.
Marshall discusses how to find out if your students are using SSR time wisely, and what to do about it if they are not.

Michaels, Judith Rowe. *Dancing with Words: Helping Students Love Language through Authentic Vocabulary Instruction.* Urbana, IL: NCTE, 2001.
Great book for vocabulary ideas.

Mitchell, Diana and Leila Christenbury. *Both Art and Craft: Teaching Ideas That Spark Learning.* Urbana, IL: NCTE, 2000.
Geared to grades 7-12, this books offers ideas for literature, reading, writing, and thematic units.

Morgan, Norah and Juliana Saxton. *Asking Better Questions: Models, Techniques, and Activities for Engaging Students in Learning.* Stenhouse. Geared K-8, this book proves that good questions lead to better learning.

Nell, Victor. *Lost in a Book: The Psychology of Reading for Pleasure.* New Haven, CT: Yale University Press, 1988.
Theoretical treatment of pleasure (ludic) reading.

Ramos, Jodi. *Elementary Minilessons: Lessons and Songs, to Motivate, Inspire and Improve Writing Skills.* Spring, TX: Absey & Co., 2000.
Music specialist, Ramos provides teachers with practical ways to inspire students to write and revise.

Ray, Katie Wood with Lester L. Laminack. *The Writing Workshop: Working through the Hard Parts (And They're All Hard Parts).* Urbana, IL: NCTE, 2001.

For grades 3-8, this book is practical and comprehensive.

Ray, Katie Wood. *What You Know by Heart: How to Develop Curriculum for Your Writing Workshop.* Portsmouth, NH: Heinemann, 2002.

Ray shows how the most effective curricula result from the teacher's deep understanding of writing.

Robb, Laura. *Teaching Reading in Middle School.* Urbana, IL: NCTE, 2000.

Robb presents a strategic approach to teaching reading that improves comprehension grades 6-9.

Schoenbach, Ruth, Cynthia Greenleaf, Christine Cziko, and Lori Hurwitz. *Reading for Understanding: A Guide to Improving Reading in Middle and High School Classrooms.* Urbana, IL: NCTE, 1999.

Describes a breakthrough Academic Literacy program piloted in San Francisco schools

Serafini, Frank. *The Reading Workshop: Creating Space for Readers.* Portsmouth,

NH: Heinemann, 2001.
Serafini focuses on reading workshop by providing theory, curricular components, and suggestions for further reading as well as sound, practical insights.

Strickland, Dorothy S., Kathy Ganske, and Joanne K. Monroe. *Supporting Struggling Readers and Writers: Strategies for Classroom Intervention 3-6.* Stenhouse, 2001.
The authors explore factors that contribute to success and failure in literacy and provide strategies for helping students at risk.

Tovani, Cris. *I Read It, but I Don't Get It.* Stenhouse, 2000.
Jam packed with practical tips that will benefit all readers. Tovani's engaging style makes for easy yet productive reading.

Weinstein, Larry. *Writing at the Threshold: Featuring 56 Ways to Prepare High School And College Students to Think and Write at the College Level.* Urbana, IL: NCTE, 2001.
The title says it all.

Whitmore, Kathryn F. and Caryl G. Crowell. *Inventing a Classroom: Life in a Bilingual, Whole Language Learning Community.* Stenhouse, 1994.

Authors explore the patterns of teaching and learning, how children invent oral and written language, and how they create the culture and curriculum of the classroom.

Windsor, Lucinda. *Grammar in Story.* Spring, TX: Absey & Co., 2000. (2 vols.)

Comprehensive lessons for all levels complete with blackline masters of the literature referenced.

Wormeli, Rick. *Meet Me in the Middle: Becoming an Accomplished Middle-Level Teacher.* Stenhouse , 2001.

Wormeli builds on his twenty years of experience to share successful strategies on everything from motivating adolescents to applying the latest brain research.

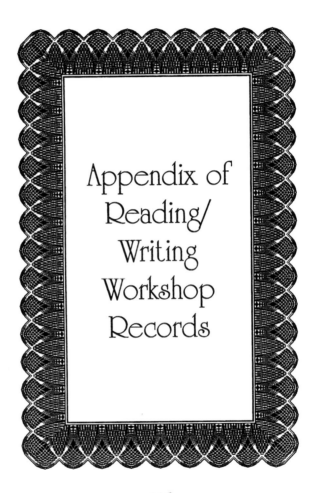

Appendix of
Reading/
Writing
Workshop
Records

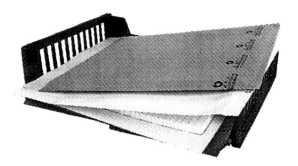

Finished Box

Genre Reading Inventory Goal

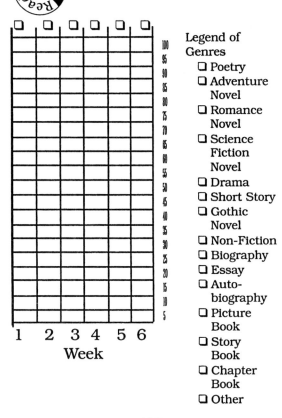

Legend of Genres

- ❏ Poetry
- ❏ Adventure Novel
- ❏ Romance Novel
- ❏ Science Fiction Novel
- ❏ Drama
- ❏ Short Story
- ❏ Gothic Novel
- ❏ Non-Fiction
- ❏ Biography
- ❏ Essay
- ❏ Auto-biography
- ❏ Picture Book
- ❏ Story Book
- ❏ Chapter Book
- ❏ Other

One-On One Reading Records

Student's Name _____

Title of Work Read _____

Date	Comprehension Skills	Fluency	Inference	Predictions	Word attack	Initial Attempts	Application	Mastery	Pages Read

Status-of-the-Class

Writing
Word
Print
Reading

Student Name	Monday	Tuesday	Wednesday	Thursday	Friday

Writing Performance Profile

Student Name _____

	Duration	Effort	Quality	Effectiveness
Prewriting				
Writing				
Rewriting				
Publishing				

Structure/Mechanics Writing Inventory

Student Name
_____

	Introduced	Applied	Mastered	Comments
FORM				
Fiction				
Nonfiction				
Essay				
Play				
Poetry				
Descriptive				
Narrative				
Informative				
Classificatory				
Persuasive				
WRITING STRUCTURES				
Lead				
Voice				
Supporting Details				
Internal Coherence				
External Coherence				
Organization				
Conclusion				
WRITING MECHANICS				
Complete Sentences				
N./V./ProN. Agreement				
Capital Letters				
End Marks				
Commas				

Reading Inventory
Goal Setting Sheet

Student Name _____

Goal	Author	Title	City: Company	Date
Number of pages to be read	Last Name, First Name	Title of Book Underlined Story in Quotes followed by Title of book or mag. Underlined	City of Pub:. Company Date	Copy-right
Example: 75 pages	Janeczko, Paul	**The Music of What Happens**	NY: Orchard	1988
Week ONE				
Week Two				
Week Three				
Week Four				
Week Five				
Week Six				

 Reading Folders
or
Writing Folders

126

Reading Memory Quire

The Eight Page Book

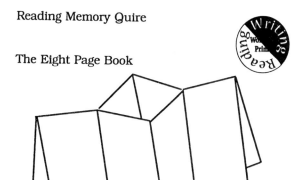

Instructions:
Page one: Title and author of reading selection.
Page two: What strikes you about the beginning/introduction?
Page three: Explain what in the story makes you think this way.
Page four: What strikes you about the middle?
Page five: Explain how the author caused this.
Page six: What about the conflict or major point strikes you?
Page seven: Explain how the words/language/diction caused this.
Page eight: What about the ending/conclusion strikes you? Explain the tone that causes this.

Portfolio Profiles

The student selects one entry from the reading category, one entry from the writing category, and one entry from the speaking, listening, or viewing categories for a total of three entries. Then the student, teacher, parent, and peer assess these entries as representative of the student's work.

Self-Evaluation Log

Monday	Tuesday
I wrote my first liter-ary letter. My mother read it, but Daddy answered back. Cool.	
Wednesday	Thursday
Friday	The Week

A Writing Workshop Center

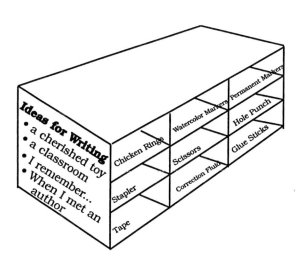

Ideas for Writing
• a cherished toy
• a classroom
• I remember...
• When I met an author

Chicken Rings

Watercolor Markers Permanent Markers

Hole Punch

Scissors

Glue Sticks

Stapler

Correction Fluid

Tape

Skills Checklist

Student Name_____

✔ Check when attempted.
✖ Check when mastered.

COMPREHENSION

Main Idea

Sequence of Events

Cause and Effect

Drawing Conclusions

Predicting Outcomes

Writing Responses

Comments:

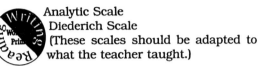 Analytic Scale
Diederich Scale
(These scales should be adapted to what the teacher taught.)

	Low		Middle		High

General merit

Focus	2	4	6	8	10
Organization	2	4	6	8	10

Depth of Development

	2	4	6	8	10
Voice	2	4	6	8	10

Mechanics

Usage	1	2	3	4	5
Punctuation	1	2	3	4	5
Spelling	1	2	3	4	5
Handwriting	1	2	3	4	5

Comments

Total ____

Analytic Scale for a Narrative

Student Name _____

	Low		Middle		High
Section One					
Focus	1	2	3	4	5
Sequence	1	2	3	4	5
Beginning	1	2	3	4	5
Middle	1	2	3	4	5
End	1	2	3	4	5

Subtotal for section one   _____

                                   x3

Total for section one   _____

Section Two					
Capitals	1	2	3	4	5
End Marks	1	2	3	4	5
Spelling	1	2	3	4	5
Handwriting	1	2	3	4	5
Prewriting	1	2	3	4	5

Subtotal for section two   _____

                                   +1

Total for section two   _____

Total (add section one and two)   _____
Comments

Notes